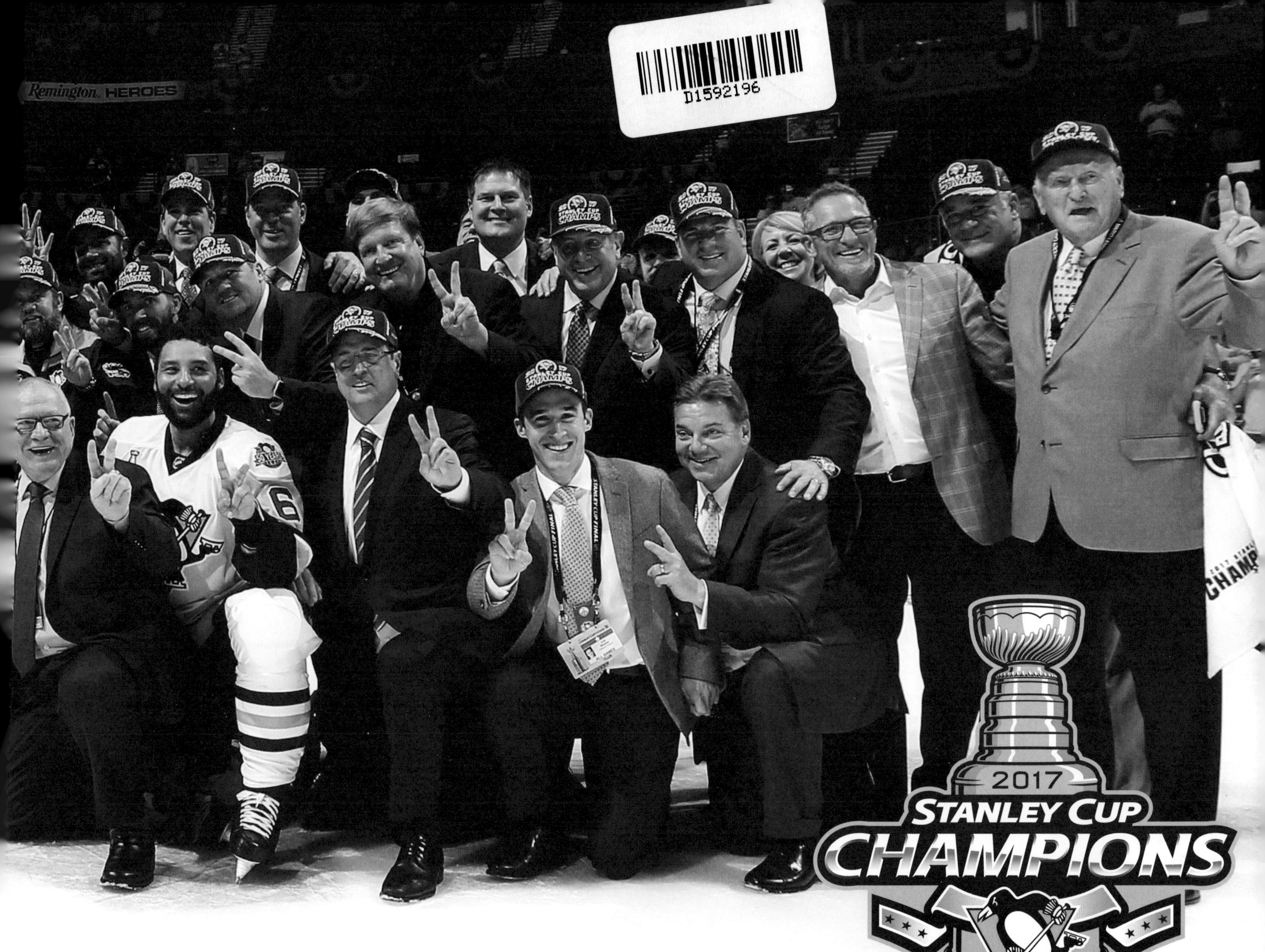
Remington HEROES
2017
STANLEY CUP
CHAMPIONS

BACK-2-BACK

THE OFFICIAL PITTSBURGH PENGUINS STANLEY CUP CHAMPIONSHIPS COMMEMORATIVE BOOK

SKYBOX PRESS • SAN DIEGO

Merci Marc Andre!
5
96.1 KISS
WDVE
Y108

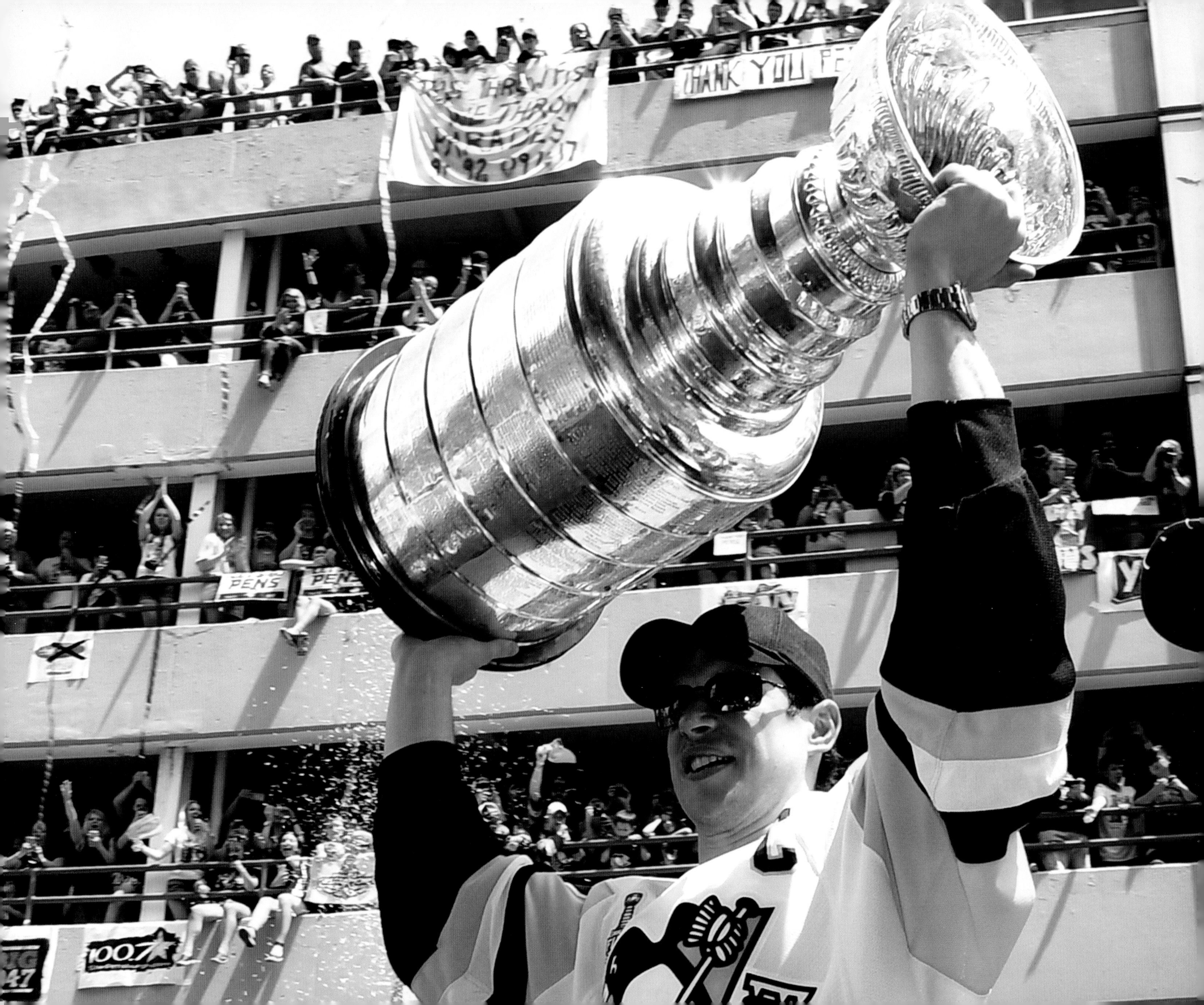
THANK YOU
PENS
100.7

37
WARRIOR

GUENTZEL
59
VAUGHN

CROSBY
87
GUENTZEL
59
SHEARY
43

SCHULTZ
4
DUMOULIN
8

87
1917
NHL
2017

TABLE OF CONTENTS

50
FLEURY
COLE
28
DALEY
6
SCHULTZ
4
MAATTA
3
CULLEN
HAGELIN
62
Reebok

ROWNEY
WILSON
23
HORNQVIST
72
MALKIN
71
KESSEL
81
KUNITZ
14

June 12, 2016

June 11, 2017

FOREWORD

PATRIC HORNQVIST

Patric Hornqvist joined the Penguins in the summer of 2014, coming to Pittsburgh in a trade with the Nashville Predators, with whom the right winger had played all of his six seasons in the NHL. Hornqvist enjoys the distinction of having scored both the 2016 Stanley Cup-clinching empty net goal against the San Jose Sharks and the 2017 Stanley Cup game winner against his former team.

In 2016, in Game 6 against San Jose, we took the lead 2-1 midway through the second period on a goal by Kris Letang. We held onto that lead, and then, with a couple of minutes left in the game, the Sharks pulled their goalie. An empty net is a different situation than a penalty kill because when a team pulls its goalie, they go up a man but you still have five guys on the ice, but when it's a penalty, you go down a man, and with only four guys you have to cover a lot more ice.

I remember Coach Sullivan calling for me, Matt Cullen, and Sidney Crosby. They are both centers, and in that situation you usually have two centermen on the ice because if there were an icing, and if the referee were to kick Sid out of the face-off circle then you need another center to take the draw.

So, the Sharks entered our zone, and they started to get a little pressure on us, and I ended up being on the left wing even though I usually play on the right. Crosby was on the left, and Cullen was down low. Then Brent Burns passed it across to Mark-Edouard Vlasic, who took a shot, but Sid blocked it. He blocked it, controlled it, and passed it all in one motion. When Burns made the pass across, I moved over to support Sid, and when Sid blocked the shot, I turned up the ice, and he slid the puck right up the middle to me.

I never made eye contact with Sid. You don't have to. When Sidney Crosby has the puck, he knows where you are. He made a perfect pass.

Brent Burns couldn't get close enough fast enough to pressure me, so I had a wide-open shot. It all happened in just a few seconds, but I remember being nervous. I remember I was squeezing my stick really, really hard. And I remember telling myself, "I can't miss this. I'm going to to score it."

And I did.

• • • • •

One year later, almost to the day, we were back in the Final, back playing a Game 6 with a chance to win the Cup, back on the road, this time in Nashville. One big difference from the year before is that Game 6 against the Predators was tied—and not just tied, but tied 0-0. When you're playing a game that is tied, say, 3-3 or 4-4, you have confidence that you can score because you've done it already. But when it gets late in a game that is tied 0-0, you don't have that same confidence, and that makes the first goal so huge.

We took two quick penalties in the middle of the third period, giving Nashville a 5-on-3. We were able to kill it, but it tired our guys out, so after that we had to play the whole bench just to get guys rest.

Then, with just under two minutes to play, I'm forechecking on our left side when Chris Kunitz gets the puck down low on the right, and he walks up the wall, so I go straight to the net to get in front of [Predators goalie] Pekka Rinne. Kunitz makes a great pass to Justin Schultz, and he takes the shot.

I try to tip it, but I miss. I know that the boards in that rink are pretty lively, not soft, so I know it's going to take a good bounce. And I see that Schultz's shot is totally straight, not wobbling, so I know it's going to come back pretty straight, not bounce toward the corners. I have to skate a little bit to get around Rinne, and I turn into the puck, and then I see it coming off the side of the net, and I see a space where Rinne is off his post, and I think I'll try to hit it in the air and off his back because I can't shoot it straight from where I am behind the net.

And I do.

The way it worked out, there was no one around me, so I got a few seconds to myself. I remember taking a deep breath and thinking, "It can't get any better than this."

And it doesn't.

PARTY
STAFF

INTRODUCTION

MIKE LANGE

When the Penguins opened training camp in September 2016 as the defending Stanley Cup champions, head coach Mike Sullivan challenged his team to become the NHL's first back-to-back winners in almost two decades. To establish a foundation for reaching that goal, he began in the preseason to deliver a familiar mantra: "Play the right way."

For the Penguins, that simple phrase packed a whole series of meanings. Sullivan wanted them to play fast and pay attention to detail, to take care of the puck so that his offensively gifted team would have it more often than not. He wanted them to play with conviction and resilience, to learn again how to consistently find their style, attitude, and identity.

Many people didn't think it could be done, citing the "Stanley Cup hangover" that had plagued so many recent champions, and sure enough, the obstacles started popping up immediately. Injuries cost captain Sidney Crosby the first two weeks of the season and starting goaltender Matt Murray the first three weeks. But Marc-Andre Fleury filled in brilliantly in net for Murray, and when Crosby returned he began to score goals at what for him was a record pace as the Penguins won 20 of their first 30 games.

In late November, with veterans Chris Kunitz and Patric Hornqvist out with injuries, young winger Jake Guentzel made his NHL debut—and scored twice on his first night, a preview of what was to come later. Playing and winning through waves of injuries was a familiar theme for the Penguins. Pittsburgh played the final quarter of the schedule without three of its regular defensemen, including All-Star Kris Letang, who appeared in just 41 games before a neck injury ended his season.

Fueled by Crosby, as well as Evgeni Malkin and Phil Kessel, the Penguins just kept scoring goals and winning games, finishing with the league's second-best record. It was feared that the Letang injury would sabotage their Cup hopes, but defensemen Ian Cole, Justin Schultz, and Brian Dumoulin ascended to a higher level, and general manager Jim Rutherford traded for veteran defenseman Ron Hainsey, who at 36 had never before played in a Stanley Cup playoff game but quickly became a valuable contributor.

When Matt Murray injured his hamstring during the warm-ups for Game 1 of the opening-round series against Columbus—literally 30 minutes before the start of the playoffs—the Penguins knew exactly how to handle it. That came not only from experience but also from following the lead of Crosby, the perfect captain to lead this team, in that he understands the game and what it takes to win. I've been around the Penguins since 1974, and the guys in this dressing room possessed a desire to win that was stronger than any I've ever seen.

No matter what happened, the Penguins found a way to win. Even better, they never bragged about it. They just went out and did it, and everyone contributed through the injuries. It was discovered later that third-line center Nick Bonino had played the final two periods of Game 2 of the Stanley Cup Final against Nashville on a broken leg, suffered blocking a shot during the first period. That summed up the Penguins' determination.

Fleury was instrumental in victories over Columbus and Washington, blanking the Capitals on their home ice in Game 7. Malkin led all scorers in the playoffs, followed closely by Crosby, who delivered a complete game night after night. Guentzel wound up leading the playoffs in goals, and Murray returned to the net in the Conference Final victory over Ottawa, becoming the first goalie in NHL history to win the Cup in each of his first two seasons. At just 23 years of age, he is incredibly poised on the big stage, a kid born to be a goalie.

By the time Carl Hagelin's empty-net goal sealed a 2-0 Game 6 victory in Nashville and a second consecutive Stanley Cup, I knew two things for sure: Elvis had left the building, and the Penguins had played the right way.

NEXUS
87
CCM
87
87
PENGUINS
87
CCM
87
PENGUINS
CCM
SAP

2016
STANLEY CUP
CHAMPIONS
2015-2016
CHAMPIONSHIP SEASON

CENTER
FEEL THE LOVE
0 2:31 0
1995-96 NORTHEAST DIVISION CHAMPIONS
1992-93 PATRICK DIVISION CHAMPIONS
WALES CONFERENCE CHAMPIONS
LUMBER
RAM
SHEETZ
SHEETZ
FEEL THE LOVE
GetGo
BAUER
CCM
PREMIER
FLEURY
29
NEXUS

REGULAR SEASON

The Penguins' sluggish start to the 2015-16 season—winning just 15 of their first 28 games—prompted general manager Jim Rutherford to act swiftly. In mid-December head coach Mike Johnston was replaced by Mike Sullivan, the coach at AHL Wilkes-Barre/Scranton. Immediately, Pittsburgh took off—but in the wrong direction. The Penguins lost their first four games under Sullivan, scoring only four goals in the process. But then the tumblers clicked, especially for captain Sidney Crosby.

Crosby muddled through the slowest start of his career but pivoted as quickly as the team. In his final 50 games, Crosby had 30 goals and 36 assists. The attack was bolstered by more roster moves, including trades for puck-moving defensemen Trevor Daley and Justin Schultz. Rutherford also added the final piece to the HBK Line, obtaining Carl Hagelin in a trade to go with offseason acquisitions Nick Bonino and Phil Kessel.

Although the Penguins would finish 16 points behind Washington in the Metropolitan Division, by mid-March there was little doubt they were the NHL's most dangerous team. Then, on March 31, goalie Marc-André Fleury sustained an injury. Heading into the playoffs, the question was whether preternaturally calm but relatively untested rookie Matt Murray, 4-0 with a .936 save percentage since replacing Fleury, could handle the playoff pressure and workload after returning from his own injury, suffered on the last day of the regular season.

Marc-Andre Fleury halted a three-game losing streak to start the 2015–16 season by turning away all 22 shots he faced en route to shutting out the Senators 2-0.

LEFT

Penguins fans are everywhere, including Arizona, where Phil Kessel heads for a warm-up skate before he scores the first of his 26 goals during 2015–16.

OPPOSITE

In his first season as a Penguin, veteran center Nick Bonino had the second-highest plus-minus of his career at +13.

WE ARE STRONGER
TOGETHER. JOIN US.
United Way
EASTON
CCM

LOVEJOY
12
BAUER
23
VAUGHN

OPPOSITE

Evgeni Malkin assisted on and celebrated Ben Lovejoy's first goal of the season, a second period score that put the Penguins up for good in a 4-3 home win against the Sabres.

RIGHT

Patric Hornqvist concentrates on the puck while providing a distraction in front of the net.

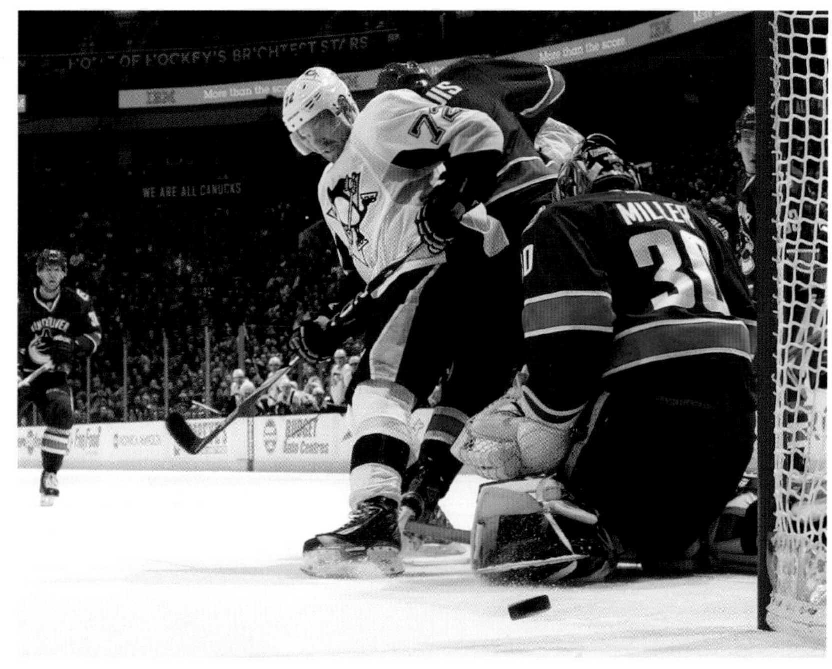

ABOVE

Sidney Crosby readies himself for a game at Vancouver. His second period power play goal helped extend the Penguins win streak to five games.

LEFT

Defenseman Rob Scuderi stretches before Military Appreciation Night.

TOP LEFT

After struggling to a 15-10-3 start, head coach Mike Johnston was replaced on December 12. In two seasons, Johnston's teams had a record of 57-38-15 and won one playoff game.

BOTTOM LEFT

New head coach Mike Sullivan was promoted from Wilkes-Barre/Scranton of the AHL and led the Penguins to a 33-16-5 finish in the regular season.

TOP RIGHT

It didn't take undrafted rookie Conor Sheary long to have an impact in the NHL, netting a goal in his second NHL game. He led Penguins rookies with seven goals for the season.

BOTTOM RIGHT

Defenseman Ian Cole handles the puck behind the net against Joe Pavelski of the Sharks. Cole was at his best in front of the net, where he tied Kris Letang for the team lead with 122 blocked shots.

OPPOSITE

Sidney Crosby takes the face-off against the Canadiens' David Desharnais during a 3-1 Penguins victory.

ESHARNAIS
51
Reebok
83
CROSBY
87

ABOVE

Acquired from the Ducks in a January 16 trade, Carl Hagelin was a welcome addition to the offense, contributing 10 goals and 27 points.

BELOW

Since joining the Penguins in 2009, left wing Chris Kunitz has scored the third most goals for the Penguins, behind only Sidney Crosby and Evgeni Malkin.

ABOVE

Injuries limited Evgeni Malkin to just 57 games in the regular season, but he was back in time for the playoffs.

BELOW

Goalie Matt Murray shows off a souvenir from his first career shutout, a 5-0 blanking of the Islanders that clinched a 10th straight playoff appearance for the Penguins.

81
BAUER
37

PLAYOFFS

FIRST ROUND

vs. NEW YORK RANGERS

After Pittsburgh split the first two games against the Rangers with Jeff Zatkoff in net, 21-year-old goalie Matt Murray tiptoed into the playoffs, needing a mere 16 saves in a 3-1 win at Madison Square Garden. The rookie would be tested more severely in Game 4, a 5-0 blowout by Pittsburgh, in which Murray registered 31 stops. The Penguins scored three first-period goals, including Eric Fehr's just 69 seconds into the game, and chased New York goalie Henrik Lundqvist after the first of two Evgeni Malkin goals. Malkin would have four points as the Penguins' power play scored on three of its six chances.

With the most anticipated series of the 2016 playoffs looming—Penguins vs. Capitals, Sidney Crosby vs. Alex Ovechkin—Pittsburgh again pounded the Rangers, driving Lundqvist from the net with a four-goal barrage in the second period of a 6-3 close-out Game 5. Since Fleury's injury, Murray, the question mark, had turned into an exclamation point, winning all seven of his starts.

Backup goalie Jeff Zatkoff gets a congratulatory hug from Phil Kessel after defeating the Rangers 5-2 in Game 1.

TOP LEFT

Patric Hornqvist scores the second goal of his first career postseason hat trick in Game 1 against the Rangers.

TOP RIGHT

Sidney Crosby beats New York goalie Antti Raanta, playing for an injured Henrik Lundqvist, to give the Penguins a two-goal lead in Game 1.

BOTTOM LEFT

Nick Bonino battles for a loose puck in Game 2; he assisted on both Penguins goals in a 4-2 loss.

BOTTOM RIGHT

Matt Cullen and Bryan Rust celebrate Cullen's game-winning goal in Game 3.

OPPOSITE

Sidney Crosby and Patric Hornqvist react after Crosby's power play goal in a 5-0 blowout win in Game 4.

HORNQVIST
72
M.STAAL
18
LUNDQVIST
30

CCM
87
PENGUINS
87
CCM
CCM
CCM

PLAYOFFS

SECOND ROUND

vs. WASHINGTON CAPITALS

While the Sidney Crosby-Alex Ovechkin matchup dominated headlines, the real story was Pittsburgh's rotating band of heroes, who provided unequalled depth in a series in which five of the matches were decided by one goal.

After Eric Fehr evened the series with a tip-in to decide Game 2, goalie Matt Murray pulled the heist of the spring in Game 3. Washington fired at will—the Capitals had a 49-23 shot advantage—but the Penguins stole a 3-2 win. In Game 4, Patric Hornqvist scored the 3-2 overtime winner, the fourth consecutive one-goal game.

Nick Bonino's 4-3 Game 6 overtime winner eliminated the Presidents' Trophy-winning Capitals in one of the most bizarre matches of the playoffs. The Penguins took three consecutive delay-of-game penalties in a span of 122 seconds in the third period, their three-goal lead evaporating in the madness. Said head coach Mike Sullivan, "I've never seen that in all the years I've been around the game."

The Capitals managed to hold Sidney Crosby without a goal in the series, but the captain contributed to the team effort that vanquished Washington.

43
CCM
72
CCM
43
CCM
CCM

OPPOSITE

Conor Sheary tries to get a shot on Washington goalie Braden Holtby in Game 2.

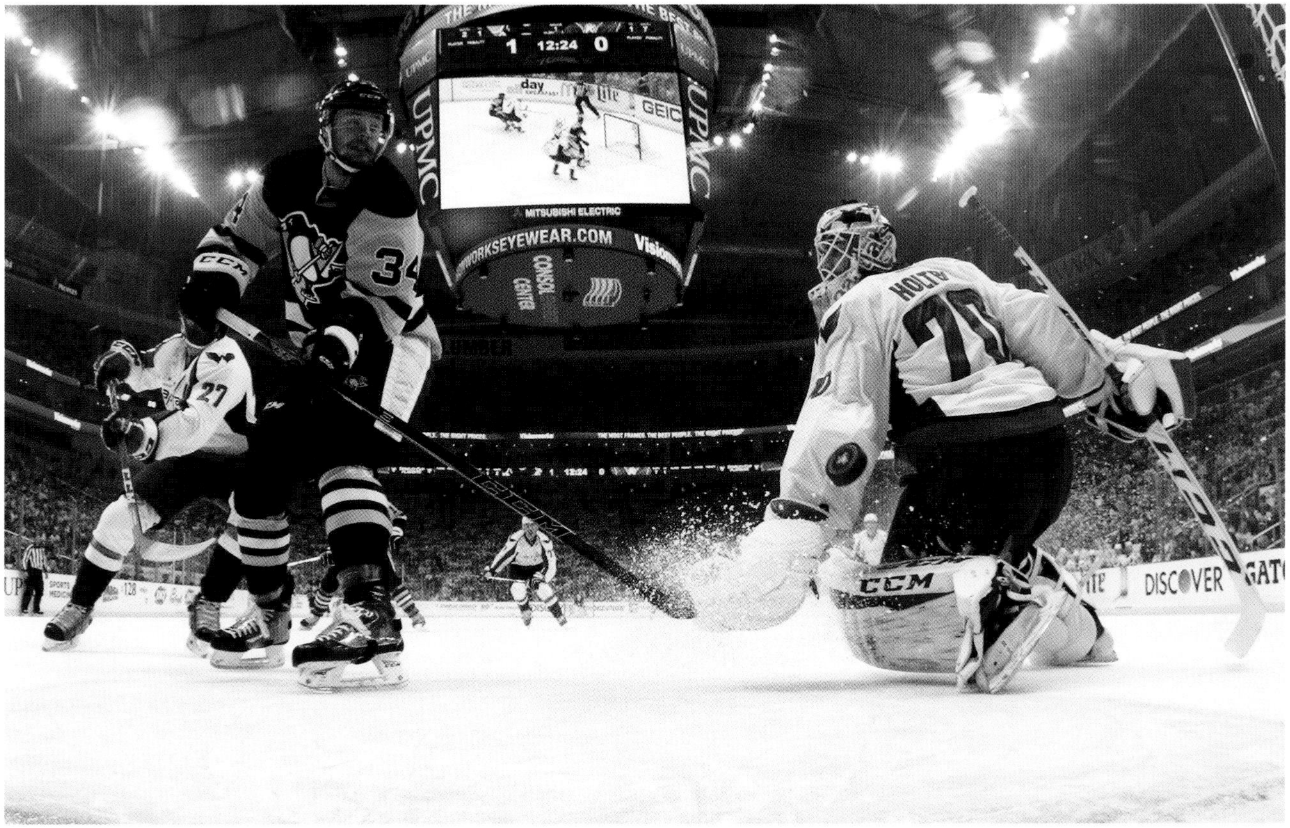

TOP LEFT

Former Penguin Brooks Orpik tries to slow Nick Bonino along the boards in Game 2, but Bonino extended his points streak to a career-high five games.

TOP RIGHT

Derrick Pouliot and Chris Kunitz fist-bump for good luck prior to Game 3. Pouliot was on the ice for two of the goals in the Penguins' 3-2 win.

LEFT

Tom Kuhnhackl lights the lamp in the first period of Game 3.

BELOW

Brian Dumoulin puts a hit on T.J. Oshie in Game 4; the Penguins blueliner also had a playoff career-high two assists.

ABOVE

Patric Hornqvist gives the Pens a commanding 3-1 series lead with his overtime goal in Game 4.

BELOW

Evgeni Malkin readies his stick prior to Game 6.

ABOVE

Carl Hagelin, second from left, *and the power play unit celebrate a second period goal. The Penguins ended the Capitals' season with an overtime victory in Game 6.*

CONSOL
HIGHMARK
UPMC
GEICO
HONDA
DISCOVER
SAMSUNG
Lite
BRIDGESTONE
DISCOVER

PLAYOFFS

EASTERN CONFERENCE FINAL

vs. TAMPA BAY LIGHTNING

The playoff spotlight had shifted to key role players GM Jim Rutherford had acquired via trade or had nurtured in the system, but Sidney Crosby grabbed it back with both hands in the Eastern Conference Final against Tampa Bay. Crosby scored three game winners: the series-tying goal 40 seconds into overtime in Game 2, which ended an eight-game goalless streak by the captain, plus two others in Games 3 and 6.

The swifter Penguins dominated while taking a 2-1 series lead through the first three games, outshooting the Lightning 124-69, but then goalie Matt Murray had his first hiccup in a Game 4 loss. After the Lightning beat Marc-André Fleury in Game 5 in overtime, Murray regained the net in Game 6, and with the Penguins on the brink, Pittsburgh played like the team that had steamrolled since January. The Penguins won Game 6, 5-2, and then controlled the clincher, outshooting the Lightning 39-17 in Game 7, with Bryan Rust scoring both goals in a 2-1 win that propelled Pittsburgh to its first Stanley Cup Final since 2009.

The Penguins get set for their fourth Eastern Conference Final in nine seasons, the most for any Eastern Conference team.

LEFT

Patric Hornqvist, Sidney Crosby, and Kris Letang celebrate Hornqvist's team-leading sixth goal of the playoffs during Game 1, which came courtesy of Crosby's franchise-playoff-record 83rd career assist.

OPPOSITE

The spotlight shined brightly on rookie goalie Matt Murray.

TODAY'S FORECAST:
NO CHANCE
FOR LIGHTNING
LET'S GO PENSH

OPPOSITE

Penguins fans enjoy a 3-2 overtime win in Game 2.

TOP LEFT

Carl Hagelin wrangles the puck from Tampa Bay defenseman Braydon Coburn.

TOP RIGHT

A fan hoists makeshift hardware while the Penguins work to deliver the real deal.

BOTTOM LEFT

Carl Hagelin, left, scores in front of teammate Nick Bonino in the first period of Game 3.

BOTTOM RIGHT

With his team facing elimination in Game 6, Phil Kessel strikes first, burying a power play goal to give the Penguins the early lead.

ABOVE

Olli Maatta shows the supreme focus needed to survive a win-or-go-home Game 7.

RIGHT

Bryan Rust gets the better of Lightning goalie Andrei Vasilevskiy not once, but twice: Rust's first goal started the scoring, and his second ended it, as the Penguins won 2-1.

OPPOSITE

The Penguins celebrate winning the Eastern Conference title and the Prince of Wales Trophy and earning a trip to the Stanley Cup Final for the first time since 2009.

FEHR
16
CULLEN
MALKIN
KESSEL
MAATTA
3
VAUGHN

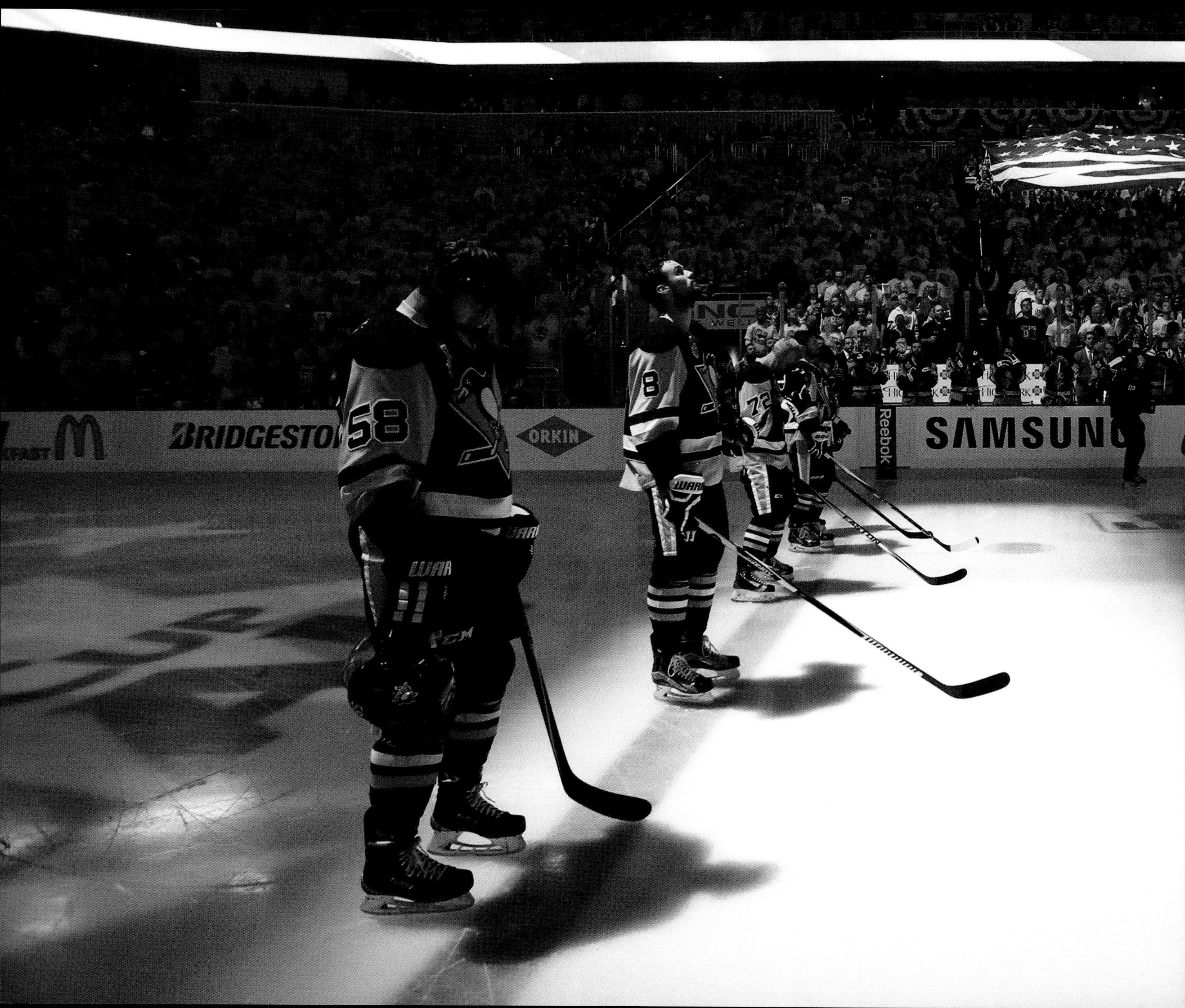
BRIDGESTON
ORKIN
Reebok
SAMSUNG

PLAYOFFS

STANLEY CUP FINAL

vs. SAN JOSE SHARKS

After Nick Bonino scored a late goal to break a 2-2 tie to beat the San Jose Sharks in Game 1, Sidney Crosby engineered a Game 2 overtime victory with some clever plotting. Crosby drew up Conor Sheary's winning goal off a face-off play in the third minute of the extra period, switching Kris Letang to the left point in place of Brian Dumoulin and positioning Sheary along the boards. Crosby won the draw and exploited a soft spot in the Sharks defense, a shooting lane that opened for Sheary after a dish from Letang.

San Jose returned the favor with a 3-2 overtime win in Game 3, then in Game 4 Evgeni Malkin buried a power play goal that proved to be the game winner. The Sharks staved off elimination, winning Game 5 in Pittsburgh, 4-2, but the Penguins throttled San Jose with a persuasive 3-1 win in the decisive Game 6, allowing only two shots in the final period. Matt Murray was 6-0 with a .936 save percentage after a loss, saving the best for last, as the Penguins and their fans back in Pittsburgh celebrated the first Stanley Cup since 2009 and the fourth for a franchise that joined the NHL in the 1967 expansion.

Sidney Crosby's spectacular résumé boasted a Stanley Cup; Olympic gold medals; the Art Ross, Hart Memorial, and Maurice Richard Trophies; the Lester B. Pearson/Ted Lindsay Award; All-Star teams; and more. His stellar play in the 2016 postseason finally earned Crosby the one missing, coveted honor: the Conn Smythe Trophy as playoff MVP.

In 2016, the Penguins extended their streak to 10 consecutive years playing in the postseason.

PENS!
LET'S GO
Reebok
CCM
58

OPPOSITE

Conor Sheary jumps into Kris Letang's arms after scoring in overtime to give Pittsburgh a commanding 2-0 series lead.

RIGHT

Matt Cullen collides with playoff scoring leader Logan Couture during Game 4.

OPPOSITE

With a 3-1 win in Game 6, the Stanley Cup returned to Pittsburgh.

TOP LEFT

Sharks All-Star Brent Burns cannot contain Carl Hagelin, who outhustled the opposition throughout the playoffs.

TOP RIGHT

Bryan Rust scored six goals in the playoffs—two more than he tallied during the entire regular season.

RIGHT

Matt Murray makes a glove save in Game 6 en route to becoming only the fifth rookie to lead his team to a Stanley Cup Championship.

HEINZ
TOMATO KETCHUP
SN
FEHR
16
HAGELIN
62
17

ABOVE

Brian Dumoulin and Carl Hagelin embrace while dejected Sharks fans look on.

BELOW

Mario Lemieux and Matt Murray celebrate their first Stanley Cups: Murray's as a player and Lemieux's as co-owner and chairman, after Lemieux won two as a Penguins player in 1991 and 1992.

ABOVE

Sidney Crosby accepts the Conn Smythe Trophy from NHL Commissioner Gary Bettman. Crosby earned the honor as the Most Valuable Player in the playoffs in part by scoring three game-winning goals in the postseason.

BELOW

Pascal Dupuis raises the Cup at the end of a bittersweet year. A member of the 2009 championship squad, Dupuis was forced to retire just weeks into the 2015 season due to a medical condition related to blood clots.

LEFT

Chris Kunitz holds the Cup for the third time in his career; he also won it in 2007 with Anaheim and in 2009 as a Penguin.

OPPOSITE

Sidney Crosby is a champion for the second time in his storied career.

STANLEY CUP
FINAL

First
STANLEY CUP
CHAMPIONS
THANK YOU
PENS!
THANK YOU
PENS!
PENS
376

OPPOSITE

Penguins fans turned out in force for the victory parade and rally on June 15, 2016.

CLOCKWISE FROM TOP LEFT

Ian Cole, left, *and Jeff Zatkoff,* right; *Phil Kessel,* left, *and Carl Hagelin,* right; *Bryan Rust; Sidney Crosby.*

SPOTLIGHT

MATT MURRAY

My first game in net in the NHL was in mid-December in Pittsburgh against Carolina. I still remember the first shot I faced: a slap shot by Jeff Skinner. It hit me right in the chest. It calmed me down. Obviously, you're nervous; you don't want to be the guy that lets in the first shot—but then I ended up getting scored on on the second shot. It was by Jordan Staal, from my hometown of Thunder Bay, Ontario.

In the last game of the regular season against the Flyers, I got injured. It was off the rush, and I read the play perfectly. I made a great save on Brayden Schenn, but then he came through the crease, and I was leaning forward, and he made pretty hard contact with the side of my head. It knocked my helmet off. I missed 10 days, but then I was back for Game 3 against the Rangers. We beat New York and then Washington, and then we played Tampa Bay in the Eastern Conference Final.

In Game 4 against the Lightning, I had one of those nights. I allowed four goals in the first two periods, and I got pulled. I wasn't my best that night, and a couple bounces didn't go our way. You know, it happens. You want to stay in and try to come back, and you obviously understand the coach isn't doing it to spite you; he's doing what's best for the team, and sometimes you need to change, and that's what happened in that game. But I always want to be in there. It doesn't matter what scenario, what score, what time of year, I always want to be in net helping the team.

I played again in Game 6, and we beat Tampa Bay in Game 7 to advance to the Stanley Cup Final. For a kid from Thunder Bay, that is like the Holy Grail. I had seen the Cup, but there is a superstition that you don't touch it before you win it.

When we beat the Sharks to win the Cup and I finally did get to touch it, Brian Dumoulin handed it off to me, and then and I was able to pass it to Bryan Rust. He is one of my best friends, so that was a very special moment for me, getting to pass it to Bryan.

Going into the off-season, I tried not to have any expectations. I really didn't know what was going to happen. I played a lot in the playoffs, and we won the Stanley Cup, but the only reason I got in there was because Marc-Andre Fleury was hurt. I knew that going into the 2016-17 season I was going to have to earn my ice time. If I was winning games, I might play a bunch in a row, and if not, I might sit a bunch in a row.

I don't let myself think too far ahead. During the summer, I try to take a break away from the game, enjoy my time off, and get ready for the next season. I think that's a big reason why we've been able to have success. The whole team has that mindset: When it's time, we'll be ready.

FINAL

71
BAUER
FINAL
Reebok
KESSEL
81

2017
STANLEY CUP
CHAMPIONS
2016-2017
CHAMPIONSHIP SEASON

2009
1992
1991
PAINTS ARENA
UPMC
GEICO
NHL FACE-OFF
50 YEARS
GNC

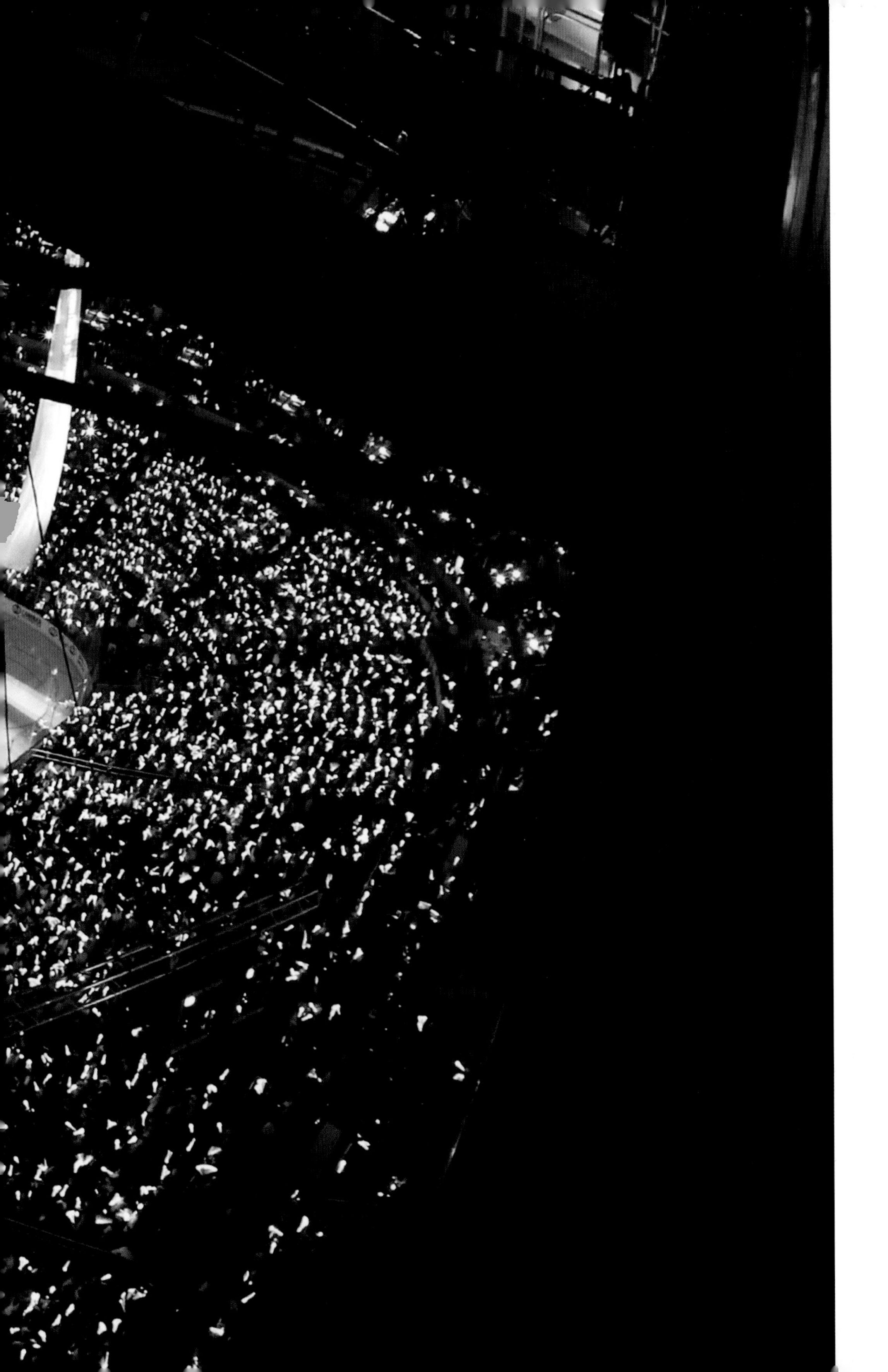

REGULAR SEASON

On October 13, 2016, in their milestone 50th season and against their division nemesis, the Capitals, the Penguins raised the banner commemorating the fourth Stanley Cup in franchise history. But there were ominous signs that the pomp of Opening Night could not conceal.

Two key players were missing. Matt Murray, the sensational rookie goalie, was out with a broken hand suffered during the World Cup of Hockey. Sidney Crosby was of greater concern. The captain sustained a head injury in a preseason practice. Fortunately, the anxiety was short-lived, as Crosby returned on October 25 and recorded eight goals and two assists in his first six games, a fabulous start to an 89-point season. Then Murray returned in November and announced himself with a blare of trumpets, winning seven of his first eight starts.

The Penguins finished with 111 points in arguably the best division in hockey; the first-place Capitals, the Penguins, the Blue Jackets, and the Rangers all finished with 100-plus points. The pressing questions leading into the playoffs were how Pittsburgh would compensate for the loss of star defenseman Kris Letang, who had sustained a neck injury in February and was lost for the season; whether the Penguins would once again oust the Capitals, who had again won the Presidents' Trophy; and whether Pittsburgh could make another magical run and defend the Stanley Cup.

On Opening Night, the Penguins raise their fourth Stanley Cup banner and commemorate their 50th season.

OPPOSITE

Phil Kessel goes top shelf against Capitals goalie Braden Holtby for the win in an Opening Night shootout.

LEFT AND BELOW

All eyes are on the prize as the Penguins watch their championship banner raised to the rafters of PPG Paints Arena.

ABOVE

Having won the Stanley Cup on the road in San Jose, Sidney Crosby thrills Penguins fans by raising the greatest trophy in sports on home ice.

KESSEL
81
Reebok
WASHINGTON
capitals
70
CCM

ABOVE

Chris Kunitz controls the puck in an early-season game against the Predators that few would have guessed would foreshadow the Stanley Cup Final.

BELOW

Sidney Crosby warms up wearing a Hockey Fights Cancer jersey prior to a 3-2 win over the Florida Panthers.

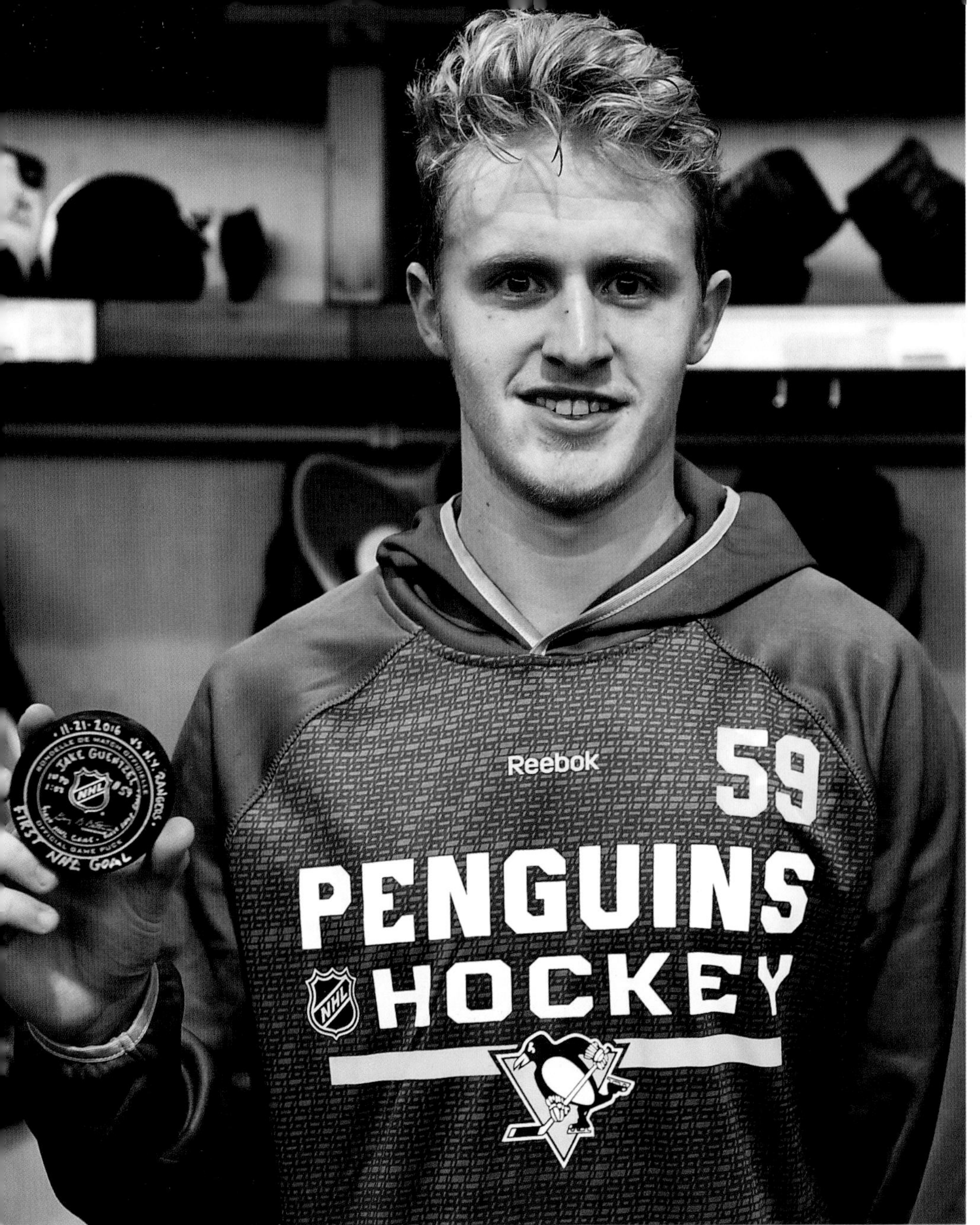

ABOVE

Rookie center Jake Guentzel holds the first of two pucks he planted in the net during his NHL debut November 21 against the Rangers.

BELOW

Matt Murray accepts congratulations after a 4-3 shootout win against the New Jersey Devils.

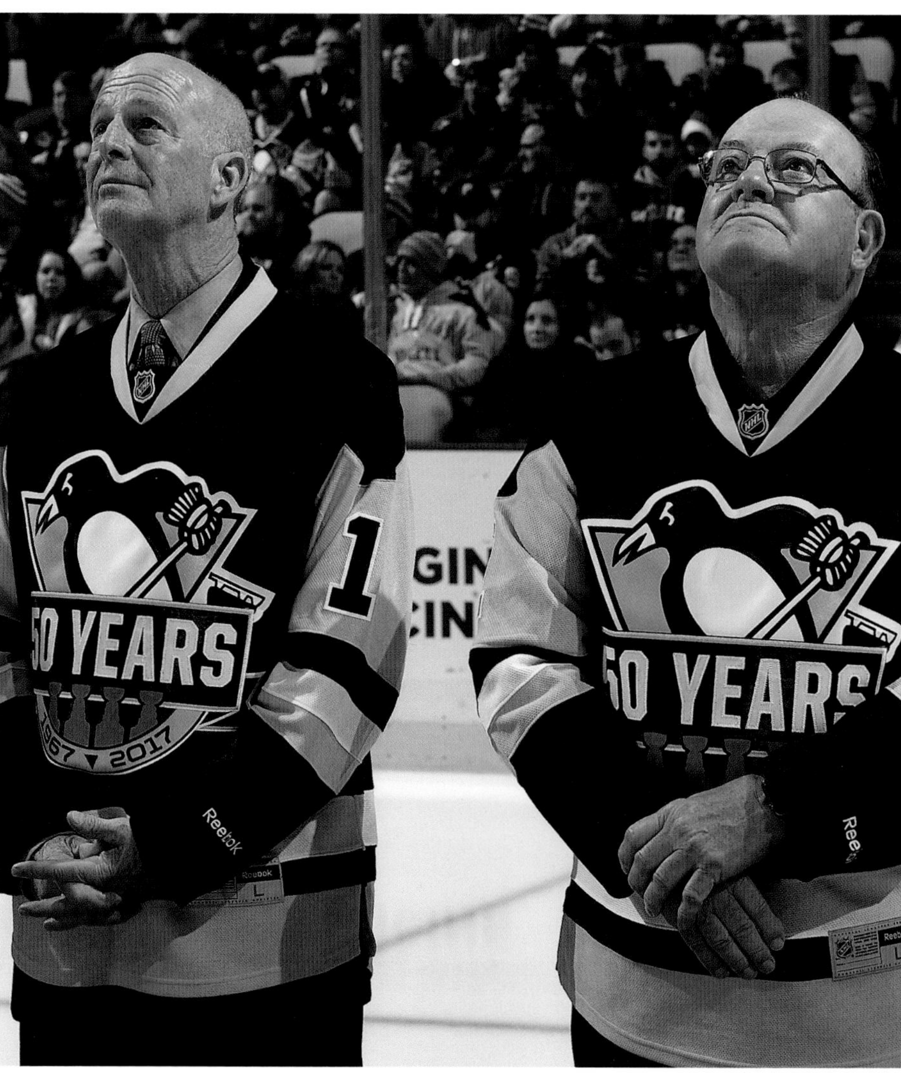

LEFT

In a pregame ceremony on December 3, 2016, the Penguins honored the 1991–1992 back-to-back Stanley Cup Champions, including Hall of Famers Paul Coffey, far left, *the only defenseman to score 100 goals as a Penguin, former general manager* Craig Patrick, middle, *and* Scotty Bowman, right, *who coached the 1991–92 team.*

OPPOSITE

Against Ottawa, Matt Cullen's 18th career shorthanded goal started a rally that saw the Penguins outscore the Senators 6-1 en route to an 8-5 win.

MAATTA
3
Reebok
CCM

Reebok
Green Mountain Energy
HIGHMARK
SHOP.NHL.COM
PPG PAINTS ARENA
87
CCM
50 YEARS
C
37
WARRIOR
8

OPPOSITE

Sidney Crosby and Brian Dumoulin sandwich Boston's Patrice Bergeron.

TOP

Conor Sheary scores with 55 seconds left in regulation against Montreal to send the game to overtime. Evgeni Malkin's goal sealed the win.

BOTTOM

Pittsburgh and Washington combined for 15 goals in a wild game between the rivals, with the Pens edging the Caps 8-7 for the win.

LEFT

Evgeni Malkin moved past Rick Kehoe and Jean Pronovost to become the fourth-leading goal scorer in franchise history.

OPPOSITE

Former Predator Patric Hornqvist puts the moves on his old mates; his first multigoal game of the season helped deliver a 4-2 win against Nashville.

energy
87
72
4
C
WARRIOR
BAUER

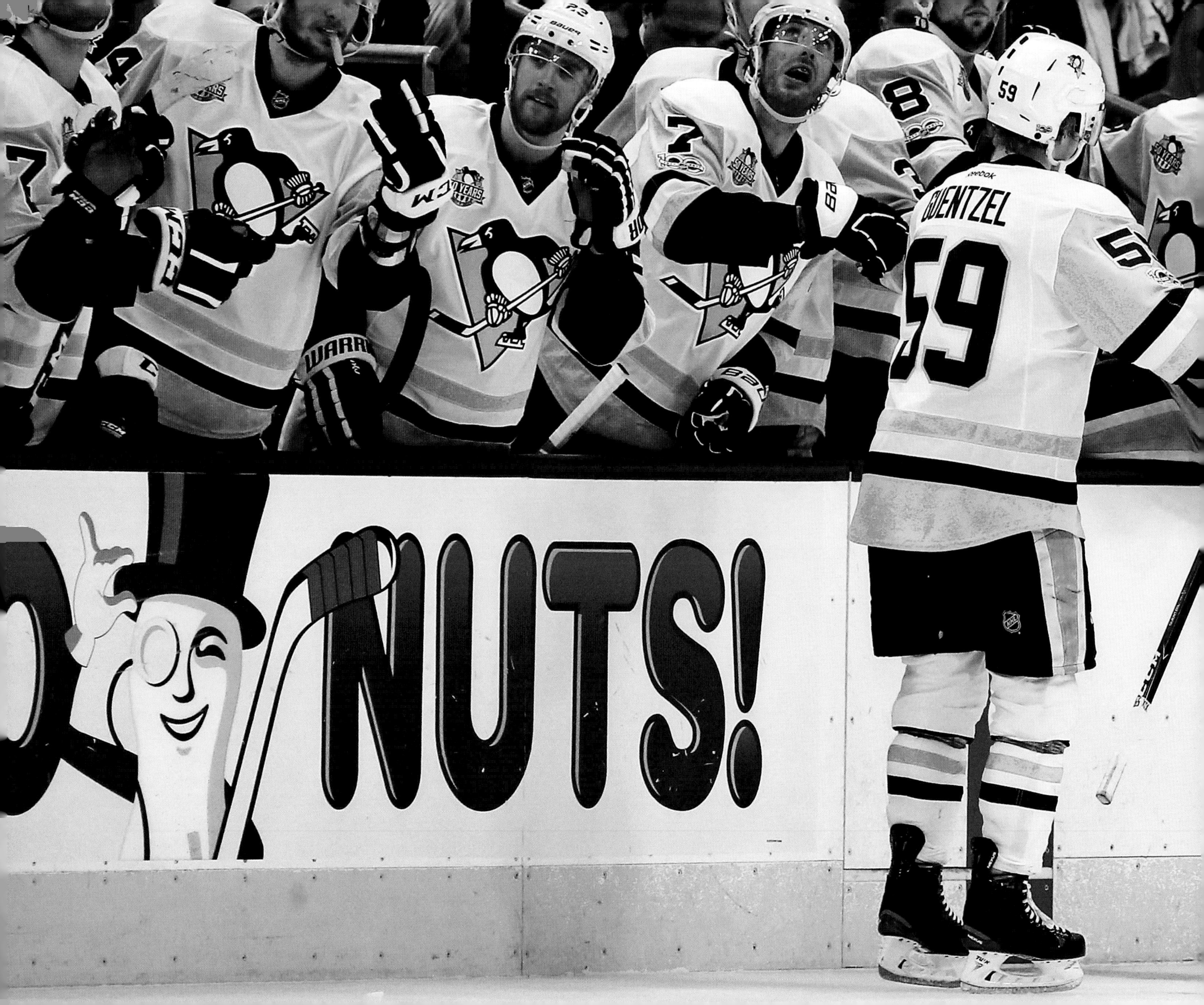
NUTS!
GUENTZEL
59

PLAYOFFS

FIRST ROUND vs. COLUMBUS BLUE JACKETS

Anything can happen in the playoffs, but for the Penguins the unexpected happened before the puck dropped when goalie Matt Murray sustained a lower-body injury in warm-ups. Marc-André Fleury, the backstop of the 2009 Stanley Cup championship team, stepped in and was superb, stopping 80 of 82 shots in the first two games, both Penguins wins. Head coach Mike Sullivan surely enjoyed grabbing the advantage over Columbus coach John Tortorella, for whom Sullivan had worked as an assistant with three different teams.

Fleury ran his streak to three consecutive wins when Pittsburgh took Game 3, but the revelation in the 5-4 overtime victory was winger Jake Guentzel, the first rookie in team history to record a hat trick in the playoffs.

After dropping Game 4, the Penguins were on the verge of giving back a three-goal lead in Game 5, but a goalie-interference penalty nullified what would have been a game-tying Blue Jackets goal. Sidney Crosby made Columbus pay, scoring on the power play, and then Scott Wilson added his first playoff goal 51 seconds later as Pittsburgh closed with a 5-2 win to take the series.

Teammates give it up for rookie Jake Guentzel following one of his three goals against the Blue Jackets in Game 3.

38
CCM
BAUER
ise
COVER®

OPPOSITE

Trevor Daley works a step ahead of Columbus's Boone Jenner.

TOP LEFT

Pittsburgh fans were confident their Penguins could defend the Cup after eliminating the Blue Jackets in 5 games.

TOP RIGHT

Sidney Crosby has a bird's-eye view of Jake Guentzel's shot getting past Sergei Bobrovsky in Game 2.

LEFT

Ron Hainsey had the assist on what proved to be the game-winning and series-clinching goal in Game 5.

MAATTA
3
Reebok
3
BAUER
CCM
CCM

PLAYOFFS

SECOND ROUND vs. WASHINGTON CAPITALS

Pittsburgh stunned the Capitals in Washington, winning the first two games with a familiar formula: solid goaltending from Marc-André Fleury, plus two-goal performances from Sidney Crosby in the opener and Jake Guentzel and Phil Kessel in Game 2. Then, five minutes into Game 3, Crosby left the game following a hard cross-check by Capitals defenseman Matt Niskanen.

Washington climbed back in the series with a 3-2 overtime win, but the Capitals could not capitalize on Crosby's absence in Game 4, as Justin Schultz scored the game-winner in a 3-2 Penguins victory. Crosby did return for Game 5 and assisted on Phil Kessel's power play goal at the end of the second period to put Pittsburgh up by one, but the Penguins clearly missed Kris Letang, their best puck-moving defenseman, as Washington scored three goals in the third to knot the series.

If the Capitals ever were going to exorcise their Penguins postseason demons, Game 7, on home ice, would have been the time. But Caps fans were sent home disappointed once more, as Fleury made 29 saves for his ninth playoff shutout, while Bryan Rust and Patric Hornqvist provided the scoring. In the end, the highly anticipated Penguins vs. Capitals matchup wasn't as much about Sidney Crosby vs. Alex Ovechkin as it was about a steadfast Pittsburgh squad that vanquished a Washington team that was unable to duplicate its regular-season success in the playoffs.

Marc-Andre Fleury allowed just 2 goals on 35 shots in Game 1, a 3-2 win for the Pens, thanks to two goals from Sidney Crosby and one by Nick Bonino.

LEFT

Forty-year-old veteran Matt Cullen, left, *started the scoring in Game 2 and 22-year-old rookie Jake Guentzel,* right, *added two goals in a 6-2 win that gave the Penguins a crucial road sweep to start the series.*

OPPOSITE

The Capitals could not stop The Captain.

90
28
28
CCM
50 YEARS
92
CCM
CCM
PREMIER
PREMIER

OPPOSITE

Marc-Andre Fleury keeps an eye on Washington's Evgeny Kuznetsov during a 3-2 Penguins victory in Game 4.

RIGHT

Ollie Matta and Tom Wilson of the Caps get tangled up during the third period of Game 4.

BELOW

Carl Hagelin checks Washington's Andre Burakovsky in Game 5; each scored first period goals in Game 5.

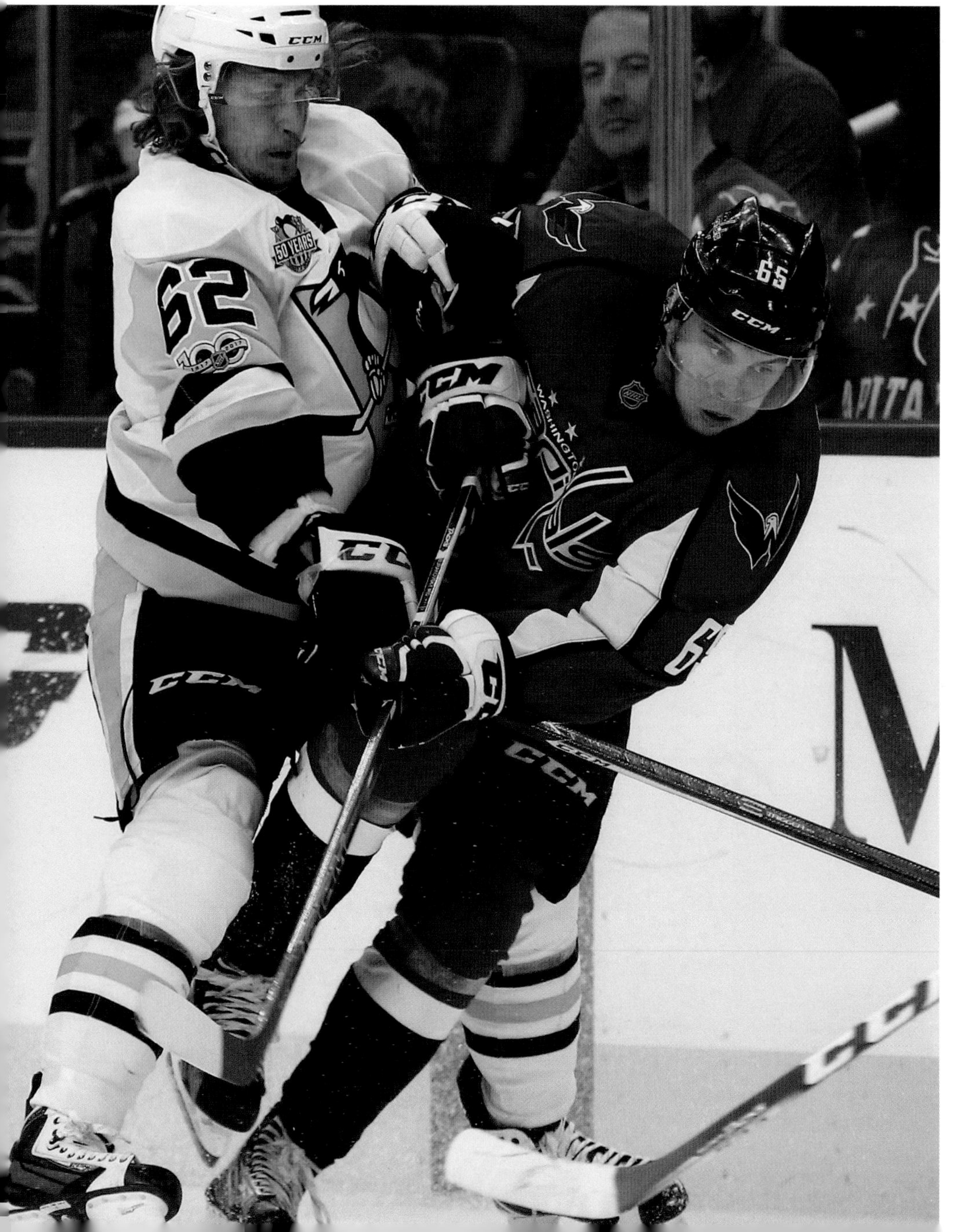

ABOVE

Ian Cole and Bryan Rust react after Rust's goal gave the Penguins a 1-0 lead midway through the second period in Game 7.

BELOW

Capitals fans do not share the Penguins players' enthusiasm after Pittsburgh eliminated Washington for a second straight year.

ABOVE

Alex Ovechkin shakes hands with Sidney Crosby, marking the end of another season in which the Capitals won the Presidents' Trophy but failed to make the Stanley Cup Final.

1991
1992
ARENA
UPMC
UPMC
LUMBER
Reebok
KESSEL
Reebok
CROSBY
87

PLAYOFFS

EASTERN CONFERENCE FINAL
vs. OTTAWA SENATORS

Ottawa had not figured in the playoff picture since losing the 2007 Stanley Cup to Anaheim, so the Senators had nothing to lose—and they played like it, jumping out in front of the defending champs with an overtime win in Game 1 and an emphatic 5-1 drubbing of the Penguins in Game 3.

After watching Marc-André Fleury allow four goals on nine shots, head coach Mike Sullivan reinserted Matt Murray in net. It was a bold but canny move, as Murray played the rest of the series, stopping 123 of 130 Senators shots—most importantly during the two overtime periods in Game 7.

Since Sidney Crosby entered the NHL in 2005, no winger has been more closely associated with the Penguins superstar than Chris Kunitz. The emergence of dynamic young wingers including Conor Sheary, Jake Guentzel, and Bryan Rust resulted in Kunitz being relegated to the fourth line. But in Game 7, Kunitz, who had not scored in the playoffs, was back playing with Crosby. The Penguins veteran started the scoring with the game's first goal, and then ended it—and the series, and Ottawa's season—with a shot at 5:09 in the second overtime to send the Penguins back to the Stanley Cup Final.

PPG Paints Arena rocks prior to the opening faceoff of the Eastern Conference Final between the Penguins and Senators.

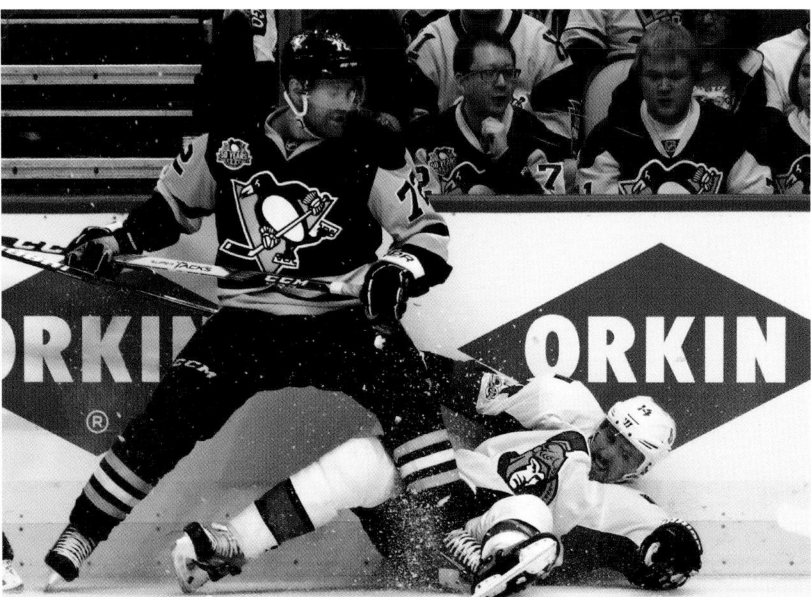

OPPOSITE

Justin Schultz dives for the puck against Senators center Jean-Gabriel Pageau.

TOP LEFT

Marc-Andre Fleury gets the start in Game 1.

TOP RIGHT

Patric Hornqvist lowers the boom on Ottawa's Alex Burrows.

RIGHT

Head coach Mike Sullivan talks strategy with Bryan Rust, Sidney Crosby, and Matt Cullen.

prise
DISCOVER
BAUER
44

PPG
PPG
NHL.com/100
71
71
14
14
CCM
BAUER
WARRIOR

OPPOSITE

Evgeni Malkin recorded an assist on the only goal in Game 2.

RIGHT

The game winner came on a third period wrister by Phil Kessel.

Evgeni Malkin, Scott Wilson, Phil Kessel, Brian Dumoulin, and Ian Cole celebrate after Dumoulin's goal, which provided the winning margin in Game 4 and evened the series.

28
COLE
28

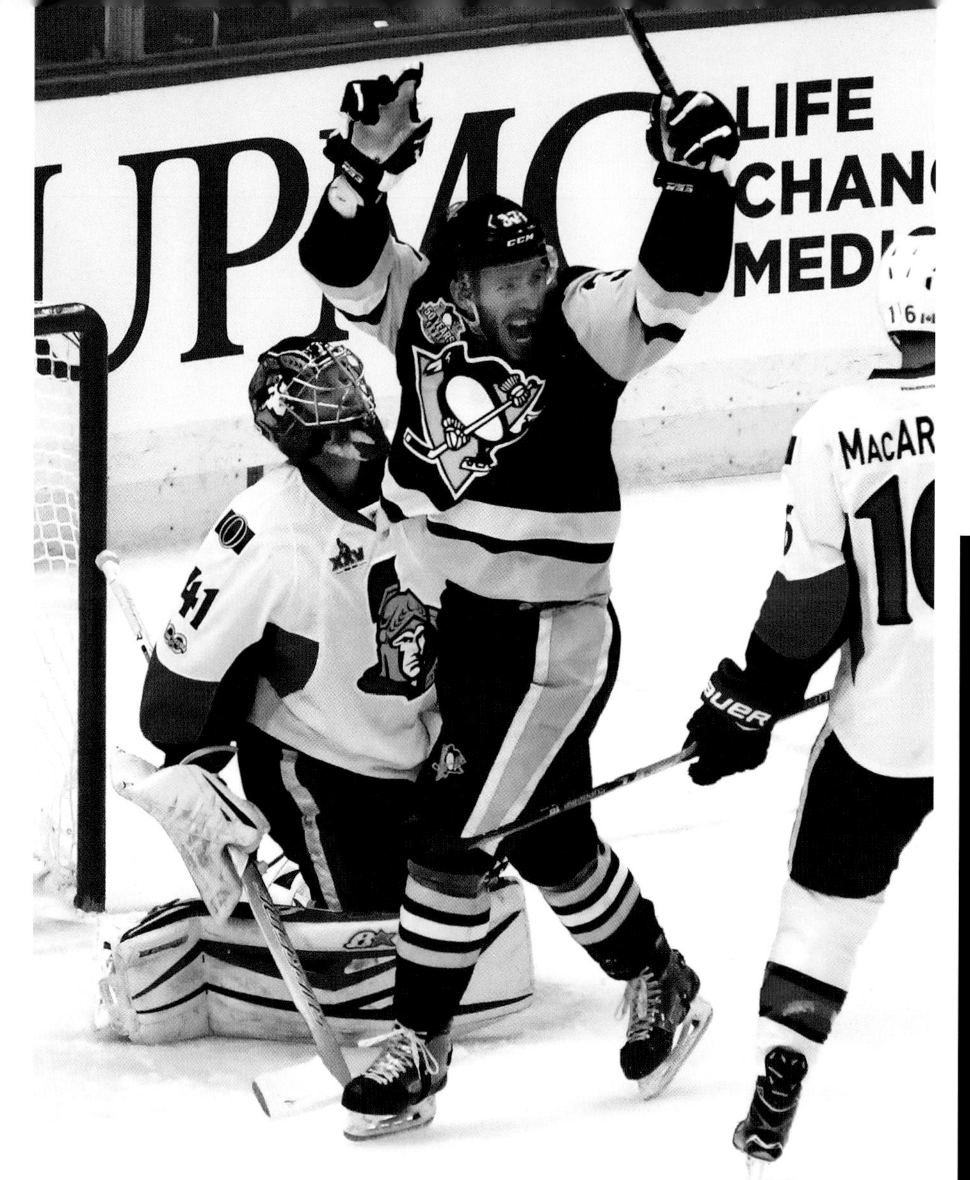

ABOVE

Carter Rowney is elated after one of his three assists leads to a score in the 7-0 Game 5 drubbing of Ottawa.

RIGHT

Matt Murray took over in net against Ottawa and recorded a .946 save percentage in the series.

OPPOSITE

Justin Schultz and Evgeni Malkin exult after Schultz's second period goal gave the Penguins a 2-1 lead in Game 7.

BAUER
71
BAUER
50 YEARS
50 YEARS
71

41
41
BAUER

OPPOSITE

Goalie Craig Anderson is on the wrong side of the puck after Chris Kunitz scored the series-clinching goal in the second overtime of Game 7.

RIGHT

On the ice and in the stands, Penguins players and fans rejoice.

STANLEY

PLAYOFFS

STANLEY CUP FINAL

vs. NASHVILLE PREDATORS

Penguins fans of an earlier generation had experienced this once before: back-to-back Stanley Cups and consecutive Conn Smythe Trophies for a once-in-a-generation player. As Sidney Crosby, in his drenched No. 87 jersey, and Penguins co-owner and chairman Mario Lemieux, in a dapper checked sports coat, celebrated on the ice after Pittsburgh vanquished Nashville in six games, it was now a fair question: Had Crosby, with three Cups and two MVPs, surpassed his boss, with his two Cups and two MVPs, as the most indispensable player in franchise history?

In Game 1, Nashville outplayed the Penguins, who endured a 37-minute stretch without a shot, but Pittsburgh outscored the Predators 5-3 for the win. Following a 4-1 Penguins win in Game 2, few expected the Predators to pounce back, but Nashville lived up to their "Smashville" nickname and thumped Pittsburgh 5-1 and 4-1 in Games 3 and 4, respectively, to even the series. Even though Game 5 was back in Pittsburgh, it felt like the Predators had the momentum, and Penguins fans wanted no part of an elimination game back in fan-frenzied Nashville.

They needn't have worried. On the first shift of Game 5, Sidney Crosby split the Predators defense and forced Ryan Ellis into taking a penalty. On the ensuing power play, Crosby set up Justin Schultz's goal just 1:31 into the game, and the rout was on. Bryan Rust, Evgeni Malkin, Conor Sheary, Phil Kessel, and Ron Hainsey all lit the lamp in a 6-0 shellacking.

Game 6 was a stalemate that seemed destined to be won by whichever team could eke out a goal. Nashville appeared to do just that in the second period when Matt Murray blocked a shot that fell in front of the open net and was poked in by a lunging Colton Sissons—except that the puck crossed the line after the referee blew his whistle, rendering play dead. The goal was disallowed, play continued, and with just over one minute left in the third period the game appeared to be headed for overtime when ex-Predator Patric Hornqvist banked the puck off of Nashville goalie Pekka Rinne's shoulder and into the net for a shockingly glorious game-winning goal.

Seventy-five seconds later, the Pittsburgh Penguins became the first team in nearly two decades to successfully defend the Stanley Cup.

The Penguins were determined to defy the odds and become the first team since the 1998 Detroit Red Wings to win back-to-back titles.

TOP LEFT

Nick Bonino ices Game 1 with an empty net goal.

TOP RIGHT

Steelers quarterback and two-time Super Bowl champion Ben Roethlisberger roots for the Pens to deliver another trophy for Pittsburgh.

BOTTOM LEFT

Ian Cole levels Nashville's Filip Forsberg, who managed just one goal in the Stanley Cup Final.

BOTTOM RIGHT

Justin Schultz and Predators winger Pontus Aberg skirmish along the boards.

OPPOSITE

Rookie Jake Guentzel is named the first star of Game 1 after scoring the deciding goal in the Penguins' 5-3 win.

SAP
DUNKIN' DONUTS
EASTON
CCM
23
52
51

OPPOSITE

With the Penguins clinging to a 2-1 lead in the third period of Game 2, Scott Wilson adds an insurance goal.

RIGHT

Jake Guentzel puts the puck past Pekka Rinne for the first goal of Game 3.

LEFT

Sidney Crosby pokes home a goal in Game 4.

OPPOSITE

The first five games of the Stanley Cup Final were all won by the home team, including the Game 5 pasting in Pittsburgh.

PLAYER PENALTY
6
0.0
0
PLAYER PENALTY
46 4:27
UPMC
PENS WIN
MITSUBISHI ELECTRIC
PPG PAINTS ARENA
PENS WIN
DUMOULIN
SHEARY
SCHULTZ
GUENTZEL
COLE
GEICO
Walmart
VAUGHN

CCM
35
FINAL
AMERICA
CCM
CCM

Scoring was scarce in Game 6, as both Nashville's Pekka Rinne, opposite, *and Pittsburgh's* Matt Murray, right, *made big save after big save.*

PENS!

OPPOSITE

Anxious Penguins fans react to the nail-biting action in Game 6 from Nashville at a jam-packed watch party at PPG Paints Arena in Pittsburgh.

RIGHT

With just over one minute remaining in the third period of a 0-0 tie, Patric Hornqvist finds the rebound off Justin Schultz's slap shot, bats it out of midair, and caroms it into the goal off the back of Predators goalie Pekka Rinne for the go-ahead score.

LEFT

Carl Hagelin seals the deal with an empty net goal with 14 seconds remaining.

OPPOSITE

The Penguins celebrate successfully defending the Stanley Cup.

STONE
KUHNHACKL
34
WARRIOR

SCHOOL of ROCK
Remington HEROES
HONDA
76

ACURA LEVEL
50 YEARS
50 YEARS

ABOVE

Evgeni Malkin and Sidney Crosby share big smiles—and three Stanley Cups.

BELOW

Matt Cullen went from preparing for retirement to hoisting Cups in consecutive years.

ABOVE

It took Phil Kessel 10 seasons to win his first Stanley Cup—and then 364 days to capture his second.

BELOW

Patric Hornqvist scored key goals that secured the Cup in both 2016 and 2017.

OPPOSITE

Back home in Pittsburgh, revelers flood Carson Street.

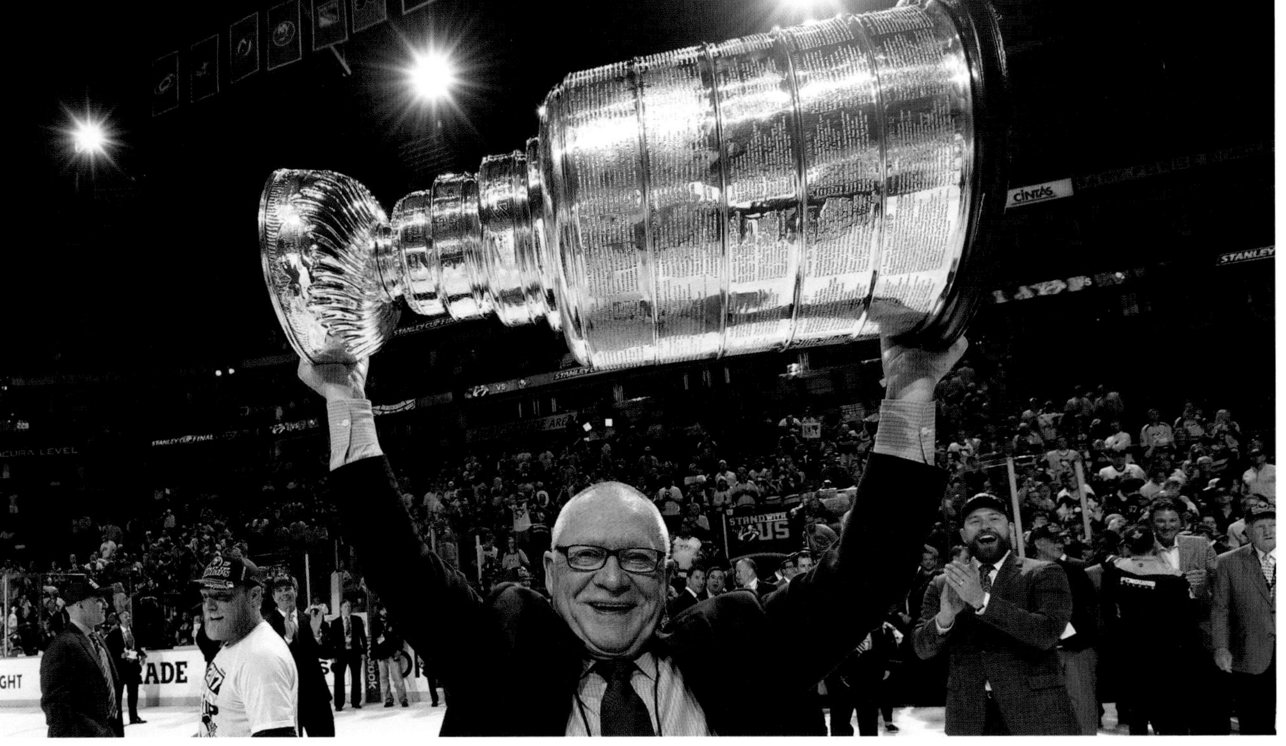

The Penguins brass with the silver Cup: coach Mike Sullivan, owners Ron Burkle and Mario Lemieux, and general manager Jim Rutherford.

LESVOS GYRO
GREEK CUISINE
THE FLATS
LETANG
PENGUINS
JAGR
CROSBY

17
66
CUP

OPPOSITE

Sidney Crosby gets doused as he delivers Lord Stanley's Cup to the locker room celebration.

CLOCKWISE FROM TOP LEFT

Coach Mike Sullivan, Justin Schultz, Mark Streit, and Olli Maatta enjoy the traditional drink from the Cup.

SPOTLIGHT

JAKE GUENTZEL

I was eating dinner. My phone rang, and I saw it was the coach calling. I was playing for the Wilkes-Barre/Scranton Penguins in the AHL, and things were going well, but anytime you see the coach's name in your phone, you can't help but wonder what it's about. I was trying to think what it could be—if I'd done something wrong, or what. Then he said, "You're going up to Pittsburgh," and it was kind of a blur after that because I had been waiting for that call my whole life.

My first game in the NHL was in late November, at home against the Rangers. I was on a line with Evgeni Malkin and Phil Kessel. Phil had played at the University of Minnesota when my dad was a coach there and I was a stick boy for the team. It's funny how that worked out.

In that first game, we were on the second shift out. It was a change on the fly, and Phil passed it to me, and I just tried to throw a puck on net and see what happened—and it found the back of the net. Sixty-two seconds: They say that is the fastest in Penguins history for a player to get his first goal. That was a cool moment for me and my family.

My locker was right next to Sidney Crosby's. He talked to me and made me feel welcome, but yeah, it was a little scary. I was just trying not to get in his way. He was on my right, so I would scoot all the way over to the left side of my locker to give him extra space. I didn't want to do anything to mess him up.

In the first round of the playoffs against Columbus, I scored five goals and an assist, and then in the second round against Washington I had four goals and four assists—but then in the Eastern Conference Final against Ottawa, I had just two assists the whole series. Sometimes it happens like that. I was getting chances, but the bounces just didn't go my way. I tried to stay positive and keep giving it my all. It was tough, but the leadership we have is phenomenal, and we found ways to win.

Playing in the Stanley Cup Final, it's hard not to be star-struck, especially as a rookie. It was such a back-and-forth series, especially Game 6. Both teams had so many chances, but when Patric Hornqvist scored with just over a minute to go, and then Carl Hagelin scored the empty net goal—I don't even remember who I was next to on the bench because nobody was sitting; we were all just going crazy.

When I got my day with the Stanley Cup, I took it to the local rink back home in Woodbury, Minnesota where I played all my youth hockey. Later in the day, I went to the StoneRidge Golf Club and played a few holes with the Cup, and afterward we had a party in a private room in the clubhouse with friends and family, and we stayed there the rest of the night.

I can't say that day was as much fun as winning the Cup—but it was close.

ATOMICdata
Making IT serve the needs of BUSINESS
We help you
move
up.
CorTrust Mortgage
WE'RE
WORTH
THE VISIT.
CITY
COUNTY

BACK2BACK
CHAMPIONS
STANLEY CUP
CHAMPIONS
LET'S GO
PENS

OPPOSITE

Chris Kunitz high-fives fans along the victory parade route on June 14, 2017.

CLOCKWISE FROM TOP LEFT

Kris Letang; Nick Bonino; Evgeni Malkin; Jake Guentzel, left, *and Conor Sheary,* right.

Reebok
CROSBY

Stanley Cup
CHAMPIONS
STANLEY CUP
FINAL
CCM
7
7

AFTERWORD

MATT CULLEN

It had been 19 seasons since a team last repeated as Stanley Cup champions. That was 1997-98. That was my rookie season in the NHL.

Playing into my 40s was not something I could have ever envisioned or imagined or even dared to hope for. When I started out, my only focus was on becoming an established, real NHL player. That's as far ahead as I ever let myself think.

I grew up in Minnesota. My dad was a high school hockey coach, so I grew up around the game. I played most of my career in places that aren't traditional hockey towns: Anaheim, Florida, Carolina, Nashville. I also played in New York, Ottawa, and my home state of Minnesota, but then two years ago, I had an opportunity to come play in Pittsburgh.

In the summer of 2015, I was expecting that my career was likely over. I was 38 years old, and I was coming off two seasons with Nashville that were enjoyable but nothing exceptional. I wasn't expecting to have a lot of opportunities. I was happy with the career I'd had, having been fortunate to play 17 seasons and win a Stanley Cup with Carolina in 2006. Truth be told, I'd have been perfectly content retiring—but I decided I would keep an open mind that summer and see what happened.

It was pretty quiet. A couple of teams called, and I listened, but then in August, Penguins general manager Jim Rutherford called and asked if I still wanted to play and if I still had the drive to play. Jim and I had history together: He signed me as a free agent in Carolina, and then, a couple of years later, when I was with the Rangers, Jim traded to bring me back to Carolina. He and I have a good relationship, and the idea of playing in Pittsburgh was very appealing to me.

I liked the idea of going to a hockey city, and I also liked the idea of being on a team with Sidney Crosby, Evgeni Malkin, Phil Kessel, and a lot of other talent—a team I thought had a good chance of contending for the Stanley Cup. Plus, I have three sons who are young and into hockey, and it was one of those unique opportunities to be around great players, to join a quality organization with a lot of history, and to be in a city where the fans really know hockey and love their team.

Penguins fans really love their team. When we won the Stanley Cup in 2016, it was estimated that more than 400,000 fans came out to the parade, and this year the crowd was said to be 650,000. That is amazing when you consider that the population of Pittsburgh is around 300,000.

I was a free agent again after we won the first of our back-to-back Cups. That summer of 2016, we went home, and I wanted to give it some time to decide whether I was ready to retire or if I was up for trying to do it again. If I was going to come back, I had to commit to the entire season and everything that goes with that—the training, the travel, the bumps and bruises. There are a lot of nights that are not so fun when you play in the NHL, and it's pretty easy to forget that when you are on a high after winning the Stanley Cup.

A big factor in the decision was the fact that we had almost our entire team coming back, which is really unique, because after a team wins a championship it typically loses quite a few guys. So, having the opportunity to go back out with the same group and try to do it again—even though history shows it's extremely difficult to repeat—was a challenge I thought would be really exciting and fun.

My first Stanley Cup in 2006 with Carolina was the most surprising. Our team wasn't expected to win anything; in fact, I think we were picked to finish 30th in the league. But it turned out to be one of those magical rides where everything went right and we wound up winning Game 7 on home ice.

Winning with Pittsburgh in 2016 was the most special for two reasons. Having been so close to retiring—I was thrilled to have won one Stanley Cup and was really comfortable with the idea of walking away—I look at that second Cup as a gift. Also, I got to experience it with my family. I was a rink rat growing up, and now to have three boys who all love and play hockey and to be able to share that with my sons, it brought me full circle.

Defending our title and winning in 2017 was the most rewarding. It is such a huge challenge, so to have found a way to keep it together and get it done is the greatest feeling of accomplishment. And to return the Stanley Cup to this city and these fans—and then to defend it—it's just incredible.

With all due respect to all the other places I've played, I honestly don't think anyone appreciates it more than the fans of Pittsburgh. The knowledge that Penguins fans have for the game and the passion they have for this team are truly exceptional.

All year long, I figured that this would be my last season. But now I'm not so sure. As I write this, I am back home enjoying the summer with my family, taking my time and trying to decide what's next. Like I say, it's pretty easy to forget the grind and focus on the glory when you are on a high after winning the Stanley Cup.

Matt Cullen with his wife, Bridget, and sons, Brooks, Joey, and Wyatt after winning the 2016 Stanley Cup.

SKYBOX PRESS

PUBLISHER
Peter Gotfredson

EDITOR
Scott Gummer

DESIGN
Nate Beale/SeeSullivan

WRITERS
Patric Hornqvist
Matt Cullen
Matt Murray
Jake Guentzel
Mike Lange
Michael Farber

COPYEDITOR
Mark Nichol

PHOTO EDITOR
Rebecca Butala How

PROJECT INTERN
Alek Weltin

SKYBOX PRESS wishes to thank Jennifer Kallas with the NHL; Jonathan Weatherdon with the NHLPA; Steve Poirier and Philip Pritchard with the Hockey Hall of Fame; Carmin Romanelli, Michael Klein, Ashlyn Barefoot, and Andy Krause with Getty Images; Linda Parker with the *Pittsburgh Post-Gazette*, Alex Driehaus and Stephanie Strasburg; Joe Halverson with Fanatics; Mike Liut, Ben Hankinson, and Robert Hooper with Octagon; and Darius and Tyge Anderson.

PHOTOGRAPHY BY GETTY IMAGES VIA NHLI:
Justin K. Aller, Pgs. 4, 5, 10, 11, 18, 19, 24, 28, 29, 30 (2), 35, 37, 38, 39, 45, 56, 57 (4), 62, 63, 65, 111, 128; **Joel Auerbach**, Pg. 24; **Al Bello**, Pg. 27; **Bruce Bennett**, Dustjacket, Pgs. 12 (2), 16, 17, 27, 30, 40, 42, 43, 50, 52 (2), 53, 84, 86, 87, 88 (2), 101, 106, 114 (2), 116; **Justin Berl**, Pgs. 122, 123 (3); **Frederick Breedon**, Pg. 116; **Mike Carlson**, Pg. 43; **Rob Carr**, Pg. 80; **Elsa**, Pg. 26; **Drew Hallowell**, Pgs. 34, 35; **Kirk Irwin**, Pgs. 6, 7, 74, 75, 105; **Matt Kincaid**, Pgs. 44, 83, 94; **Francois Lacasse**, Pg. 25; **Francois Laplante**, Pgs. 92, 93; **Jeanine Leech**, Pgs. 14, 123; **Patrick McDermott**, Pgs. 32, 33, 80, 84, 85; **Ronald C. Modra**, Pg. 66; **Christian Petersen**, Pgs. 20, 50, 126; **John Russell**, Pgs. 100 (2), 104; **Jamie Sabau**, Pgs. 94, 96; **Dave Sandford**, Dust jacket (4), front and back endsheets, Pgs. 8, 9, 46, 47, 53, 59, 103, 115, 119 (2); **Joe Sargent**, Dust jacket, Pgs. 2, 3, 48, 66, 67 (2), 68 (2), 69, 70, 71 (2), 73, 77 (2), 82, 90, 91, 95, 97, 102, 112, 113, 116, 118, 119 (2), 124, 125; **Gregory Shamus**, Pgs. 21, 22, 23, 24, 26, 30, 35, 36 (2), 37, 41, 43 (2), 44, 54, 55, 60, 61, 64 (3), 76, 77, 88, 89, 100 (2); **Jared Silber**, Pg. 31; **Ezra Shaw**, Pgs. 49, 50; **Patrick Smith**, Dust jacket, Pgs. 78, 79, 81, 85, 107, 109, 110, 115; **Mike Stobe**, Pg. 72; **Jeff Vinnick**, Pg. 23 (2); **Rocky W. Widner**, Pgs. 24, 51;

PAGE 121: Walt Neubrand/Hockey Hall of Fame (2)

www.skyboxpress.com
info@skyboxpress.com
(877) 632-8558

Skybox Press is an imprint of Luxury Custom Publishing, LLC

ISBN: 978-0-9906671-3-1

Printed in the United States of America

10 9 8 7 6 5 4 3 2 1

Published by Skybox Press, an imprint of Luxury Custom Publishing, LLC.

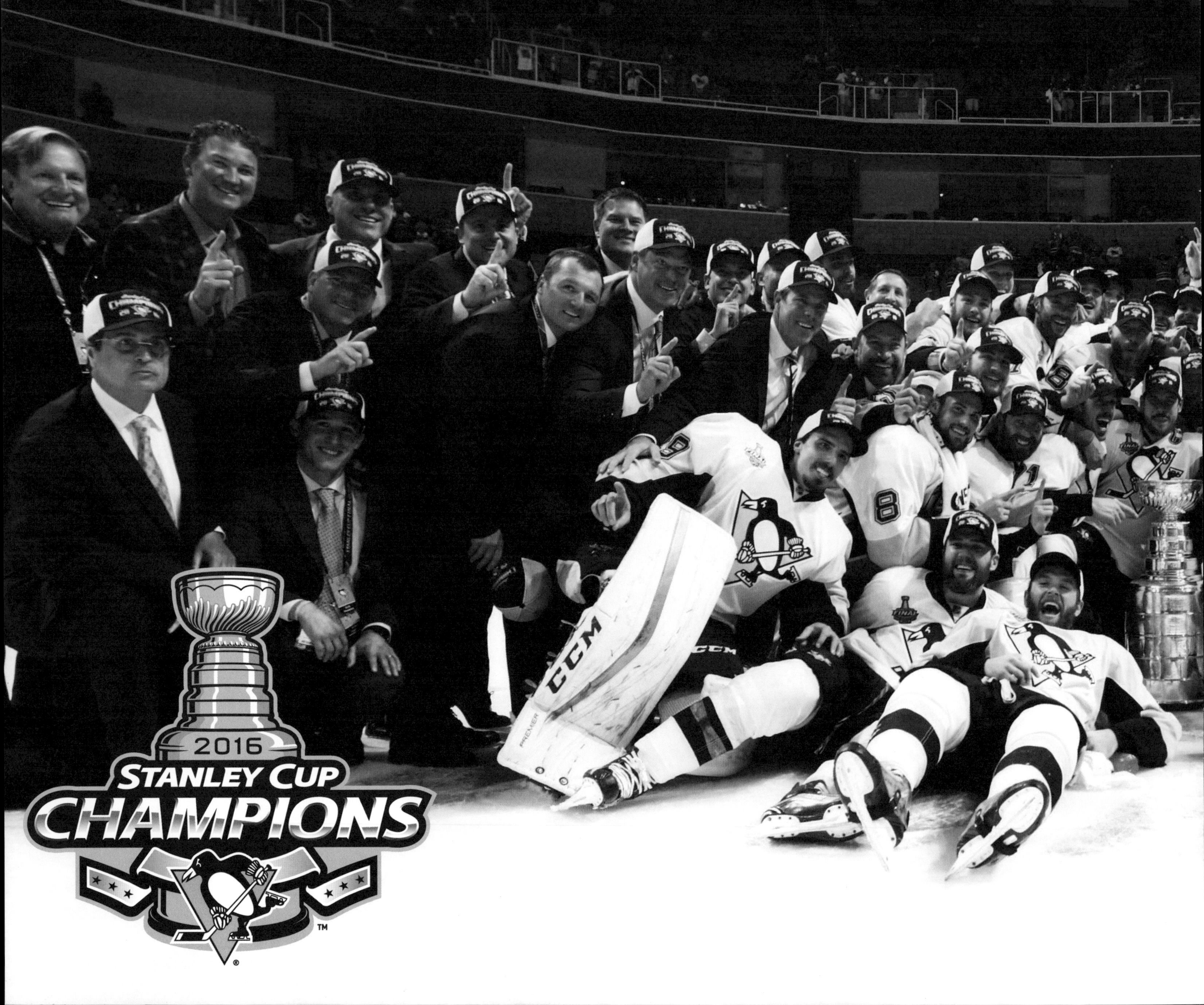
2016
STANLEY CUP
CHAMPIONS
CCM